T0157504

Essential Oils for Helping Horses

Patrica L. Wells

BALBOA.
PRESS

A DIVISION OF HAY HOUSE

Balboa Press books may be ordered through booksellers or by contacting:

Balboa Press
A Division of Hay House
1663 Liberty Drive
Bloomington, IN 47403
www.balboapress.com
1 (877) 407-4847

Print information available on the last page.

ISBN: 978-1-5043-6128-6 (sc)
ISBN: 978-1-5043-6129-3 (e)

Library of Congress Control Number: 2016915315

Balboa Press rev. date: 10/31/2016

Disclaimer

This book does not replace veterinary care. It is meant to promote a bridge between holistic animal healthcare and veterinary medicine.

The author and publisher shall have neither liability nor responsibility to any person or entity with respect to any loss or damage caused or alleged to be caused directly or indirectly by the information contained in this book.

This book is only a guideline, for horse owners to use on their horses only. It is not a training manual.

This is not a complete list of oils or their uses. It is a starting point for personal use and analysis.

Dedication

I would like to dedicate this book to all the horses I've worked on. Without them this book wouldn't have been possible. Just to name a few Doll, Stix, Levi, Flash, Skinner and Rusty. Each and every horse was a tremendous help. To their owners, a very special thank you.

I wish to personally thank my family and friends for their inspiration and support in creating this book. To my son and daughter-in-law Rob and Jen Wells, a heartfelt thank you. Without you this book wouldn't have been published. My Granddaughter Jessica Hei, thank you for the creative design for the cover.

Contents

Introduction of Essential Oils

Essential oils have been around many years. They were man-kinds first medicine.

Essential oils are the volatile liquid distilled from various parts of a plant. This includes roots, stems, bark, seeds, etc. In other words, the whole plant. Everything affects therapeutic-grade essentials oils, where they are growing, such as the soil, fertilizer, region, climate, altitude, harvest, and even the distillation process.

For that reason, the information in this book is based on using certified pure therapeutic-grade essential oils. Anything less may not give you the same results and could be harmful.

Horses and Essential Oils

Horses are a forage animal. Horses in the wild, such as the wild Mustangs, know when their body is out of balance. They will seek out what they need to keep their body balanced.

Horses today do not have the luxury of seeking out what they need to keep their bodies balanced. They are kept in barns, small areas, etc., and this is why certified pure therapeutic-grade essential oils are so important.

Aroma Therapy

Aroma therapy is smelling. The technical term for smelling is olfactory. The olfactory system is a good avenue to help balance the horses body, so letting the horse smell them and inhale them is one way to use essential oils. This method is shorter lived than oils applied to the skin. Apply to hands to activate *(see applying oils)* and then offer to horse from about 1 foot away. Slowly move closer, the horse may come to you.

Topical Application

Topical application is an essential oil applied directly to the skin. The essential oil is then absorbed into the bloodstream.

Safety and Precaution Guidelines

Keep out of reach of children.

Buy certified, pure, therapeutic-grade essential oils.

Less is more. Never exceed the recommended dose. Horses are very sensitive to the oils.

Do not apply oils around the eyes, genitalia, mouth or inside the nostrils or down in the ear.

Do not apply oils directly on the horse. Always put the oils in your clean hand first.

Make sure bottle has a dropper insert. This way you can control how much you use.

Clean the top of the bottle after each use.

Clean injury site thoroughly before use of oils on or around the wound.

Know your horses' history before picking out what oils to use. For example, pregnant, colic, pulled muscle, etc. Always consult a veterinarian if unsure of underlying problem.

Always store bottles standing upright, with the lid tight, in a cool dry place. Never store in sunlight, heat, or refrigerator.

Always use a good carrier oil such as fractionated coconut oil.

If your horse has an irritation or sensitivity to the oils, use a carrier oil to dilute. Apply oil where tack goes, only if the horse will not be ridden for 8 to 12 hours. Blistering can occur otherwise.

Phototoxicity is a reaction that occurs after oil is applied and the horse is then exposed to the sun. Mainly citrus oils cause this, but some non-citrus oils can also cause this. Always dilute these oils with a carrier oil. Grey or white horses are the most sensitive to this, and can have an adverse reaction when oil is applied around the muzzle.

Some oils are toxic. This does not mean they cannot be used, but that they need a very high dilution. Some oils can be very hazardous, but to my knowledge I have stayed away from these. Again, know your oils; your horse's safety could depend on it.

Using Essential Oils

Application Key:

A - Aromatic / Inhalation

D - Dilute

N - Neat / no dilution necessary

T - Topical-use on body

* - Avoid sunlight for up to 12 hours after use.

** - Avoid sunlight for up to 24 hours after use.

Applying Oils

To check for irritation, place a drop of oil behind the ear. Do not put the drop of essential oils directly into the ear. When testing, still use the guidelines listed below before applying the oils to your horse.

Cup your hand and place oil in palm. Place other palm on top and move in a clockwise motion to activate the oil.

If using a carrier oil place the carrier oil in palm first, then add the essential oil and activate as above. Dilution of most oils is one part of the chosen oil to five or ten parts of the carrier oil. Some oils will need more dilution with a carrier oil, some will not. One or two drops is all you need. If doing a large area such as the hips, mix with carrier oil. It can be harmful if you use excess oils.

Most can be used full strength as a spotting oil. For use as a spotting oil, first activate then place one finger in oil, then separate hair and place on skin. This works well on problem areas.

Aroma therapy oils are used full strength.

Keep in mind the different types, temperament, size, and skin types of horses. Always treat each one as an individual. It is better to use less oil and have to repeat. If the essential oil is too concentrated, the horse may not be able to cope with it.

Single Oils

This is just a guideline for how I am using the oils. These oils have more properties than I have listed.

Basil
Basil helps relieve sore and fatigued muscle. When inhaled, it will help with mental alertness.

Anti-inflammatory, stimulant.

A, D, T

Bergamot
Bergamot helps relieve itching, relaxes the body and lifts the spirit and helps clear the throat. It helps with skin tumors known as Sarcoids.

Anti-inflammatory

A, D, T, **

Black Pepper

Black pepper is a deep muscle relaxant. This is an excellent oil to massage into the horse when they are chilled (cold and/or wet). It can help pull toxins, be helpful with colic and blood circulation.

Antibacterial, antiseptic.

D, T (Always dilute with carrier oil)

Clary Sage

Clary Sage is not to be used on pregnant mares. It provides relaxation during heat cycles. As a deep muscle relaxant, it helps with muscle fatigue. It can also help with C.O.P.D symptoms.

Antifungal, antiseptic, gentle sedative.

A, D, T

Clove

Clove is an excellent oil to help stimulate the immune system. It can be used on wounds, but I prefer to use different oils.

Antibacterial, antiviral, antioxidant.

A, D, T

Eucalyptus

Eucalyptus is used for respiratory problems. It helps clear the sinus, throat or chest airways. It can also be used on over exercised muscles.

Stimulant, antiviral.

_A, D, T_

Frankincense

Frankincense is used for emotional and spiritual balance, wounds, scarring and lost of a companion. Use when a horse has lost their companion. It is also helpful to ease breathing, and is soothing to throat and chest.

Anti-inflammatory, immune stimulant.

_A, D, T_

Geranium

Geranium is used for the nervous system, hormonal balancing, relaxing and calming. It is also used for bruising and is an insect repellent.

Antibacterial, antidepressant.

_A, D, T_

Ginger

Ginger is used for warming and stimulating the circulatory system. It is another oil to use on wet and cold horses. It is soothing to the joints and arthritic joints. This oil will help ease congestion and tightness.

Analgesic, antiseptic, anti-catarrhal.

_A, D, T,_*

Grapefruit

Grapefruit is used for stiffness, fatigue, and lactic acid build-up in the muscles. It is good for a nervous, or flustered horse such as before traveling, competition, etc. It helps to bring stomach enzymes back to normal. It can be used when immediate sun exposure cannot be avoided.

Antibacterial, antiseptic.

_A, D, T_

Helichrysum

Helichrysum is an excellent choice to help stop bleeding and start the healing process from the inside out. It reduces swelling, bruising and heals wounds from the inside out. This oil helps with stopping pain. It is also an expectorant and helps promote the removal of mucous.

Anti-catarrhal, antispasmodic.

_A, T_

Lavender

Lavender is a good all-around oil. It works on wounds, the respiratory system and helps heal infections and is pain relieving. This oil can be used as a natural fly repellant.

Antidepressant, anti-inflammatory, antispasmodic, a sedative.

_A, T_

Lemon

Lemon is used to promote physical energy, healing and helps relieve muscular spams. This oil is a regulatory oil that can be used to bring down a fever or bring the temperature back up if it is low. It also helps to strengthen the hoof. Use on the throat and chest to ease breathing.

Antiseptic.

_A, D, T, *_

Lemongrass

Lemongrass will help repair ligaments and tissue. It is also good for muscles, bones and is a pain reliever.

Anti-inflammatory, analgesic.

*A, D, T, **

Marjoram

Marjoram is NOT to be used on pregnant mares. Use this oil on stiff joints, spasms, and muscular problems. Marjoram produces warmth for cold or wet horses. This oil has a sedative effect to help calm or ease anxiety and does have a laxative effect.

Antiseptic, antispasmodic, analgesic.

D, N, T

Melaleuca

Melaleuca can be used for many different things such as cuts, sores, lice, mites, strep, staph infection, and thrush.

Antifungal.

D, N, T

Myrrh

Myrrh can be used for coughs, ringworm, wounds, and arthritic conditions. Use on throat and chest to ease breathing with a soothing warmth.

Anti-inflammatory, antiviral.

_T_

Patchouli

Patchouli will relieve itching, bug bites, wounds, and bruises. It is also good on clover burns.

Anti-inflammatory and antiviral.

_T_

Peppermint

Peppermint is a good all-around oil and will help with alertness, bones, pain relief, itching, arthritis, circulation, muscles and colic. It helps with the throat, chest, and sinuses for breathing.

Anti-inflammatory, analgesic.

_A, D, T_

Roman Chamomile

Roman Chamomile promotes calmness, relaxation, and helps ease muscle soreness and spams. This oil is a good choice for animals found in shelters or rescues.

Anti-inflammatory.

_A, T_

Rose

Rose works on nervous horses. It calms, eases tension and relieves stress. Good for eye infections. It is one of the oils you can use on the eyes, if diluted with one drop in a cup of warm water.

Anti-infectious.

_A, D, T_

Rosemary

Rosemary is good for muscle pain and is a circulatory stimulant. It is good for arthritis, rheumatism and dispels fluid retention.

Antispasmodic.

_D, N, T_

Sandalwood

Sandalwood is very similar to frankincense in regards to fear related problems. This oil works after a workout, helping muscle and joint issues. This oil can be used in the eyes, diluted with one drop in a cup of warm water. Sandalwood will also help with throat and upper respiratory issues.

Anti-catarrhal.

_A, D, T_

Vetiver

Vetiver helps with unpredictable behavior or settles the horse into a new place. By grounding emotional or nervous tension, it helps with stress, or recovering from emotional trauma and shock. It can be used for arthritic conditions, muscles, rheumatism, skin care and swelling.

Anti-inflammatory, antiseptic, antispasmodic, immune-stimulant.

_A, D,_

White Fir

White fir works for aches, pains and muscle fatigue, or bone pain. This is an oil to use when your horse will be in the sun. It can help with fevers and supports blood health.

Antiseptic, Analgesic

A, D, N, T

Ylang–Ylang

This essential oil is deeply relaxing and soothing. It can also promote hair growth.

Antidepressant

A, D, T

Don't be afraid to blend oils. It is important to be aware of whether your oil is a Base note, Middle note or Top note.

Base Notes – Such as Frankincense, Myrrh, Sandalwood and Vetiver will evaporate the slowest.

Middle Notes – Such as Geranium, Helichrysim, Lavender and Peppermint are in between and a combination of base notes and top notes.

Top Notes – Such as Bergamot, Grapefruit, Lemon and Lemongrass evaporate the fastest.

Blended Oils

I prefer to mix my own blends, but listed below are a few blends that I have used.

Soothing Blend

For muscle cramps, arthritis, bone pain, bruising and muscle pain.

Digestive Blend

For colic and parasites.

Calming Blend

For calming. *(I have clients that used this blend when riding colts.)*

Essential Oils for Specific Use

Disclaimer: This is just a guideline to assist your horse in cooperation with veterinary care.

Allergies: Lavender, Lemongrass

Arthritis: Helichrysum, Vetiver

Anxiety: Lavender, Serenity

Bleeding: Helichrysum, Geranium

Blisters: Lemongrass

Bones: White Fir

Bruises: Geranium

Circulation: Rosemary, Geranium,
                      Lemongrass,
                      Peppermint, Pepper

Cuts: Helichrysum, Lavender

Depression: Rose, Geranium

Ear Mites: Peppermint

Fear:	Basil, Bergamot, Frankincense, Lavender, Ylang-Ylang
Fever:	Peppermint, Lemon
Focus:	Frankincense, Peppermint, Sandalwood
Founder:	Frankincense
Grief:	Lavender, Roman Chamomile, Frankincense
Hive:	Peppermint, Lavender, Vetiver
Itching:	Bergamot
Joints:	White Fir, Lavender, Sandalwood
Muscles:	Black pepper, Clary Sage, Geranium, Ginger, Grapefruit, Lavender, Lemongrass, Marjoram, Peppermint, Roman Chamomile, Sandalwood, Vetiver
Nervousness:	Bergamot, Helichrysum Lavender, Ginger, Vetiver, Sandalwood
Pain:	Helichrysum, Peppermint, Lavender
Parasites:	Digestive Blend, Lemongrass

Respiratory:	Frankincense, Peppermint, Sandalwood
Saddle Sores:	Helichrysum
Swelling:	Rosemary can be used neat for Swelling.
Trauma:	Bergamot, Lavender, Frankincense, Calming blend
Tumors:	Bergamot, Frankincense with Lavender

Recipes

Remember, essential oils **DO NOT** replace traditional veterinary care. Here are some recipes I find helpful. Know your horse and the oils you are using. All recipe amounts can vary according to weight, age, sex of horse and problems a horse has. Always activate the oils before applying to your horse. AGAIN, KNOW YOUR OILS.

Bones

Geranium – 1 drop

Sandalwood – 1 drop

White Fir – 1 drop

Fractionated Coconut Oil – 10 to 15 drops

Know your horse, you may only need 1 or 2 of these oils. You may also need to add something for muscles like a drop of Ylang-Ylang, one drop of Roman Chamomile or one drop of Clary Sage.

Colic

Bergamot – 7 drops

Black Pepper – 4 drops

Helichrysum – 10 drops

Lemon – 5 drops

Peppermint – 10 drops

Rosemary – 5 drops

Fractionated Coconut Oil – Dilute as needed

Apply to both sides of the belly below the ribs, all the way back towards the hips and continue into the flank area.

Hoof Conditioner (per hoof)

To see if you may have inflammation in the hoof, you should wet both front hooves or both hind hooves. If one hoof dries out faster than the other, it may have inflammation. Check with your veterinarian.

Frankincense – 1 drop

Geranium – 1 drop

Lavender – 1 drop

Lemon – 1 drop

Myrrh – 1 drop

Fractionated Coconut Oil – 5 drops

Lift hair and place on cornet band with thumb in a downward direction. Apply as needed.

Leg Swelling

Lemongrass – one drop (avoid sunlight)

Rosemary – one drop (this oil can be used neat or mixed when using on a large area)

Fractionated Coconut Oil – 5 drops.

Muscle Wash

Mix with fairly warm water in a bucket, then sponge on problem area. Don't be afraid to mix oils. Remember, water makes oils warmer and penetrates deeper. You do not have to add the same amount of oils.

Decide what your horse needs and which oils are best suited to accomplish this. Use one or two of the oils listed below. I like to use between 1 and 10 drops of these oils. Peppermint and Sandalwood are a good mix.

Black Pepper	Deep muscle relaxant, this is a very warming oil. When it is hot outside you may not want to use this oil. This oil will disperse toxins.
Clary Sage	Good for stiff joints, aches, pains and works as a sedative. Do not use on a pregnant mare.
Geranium	Good for bruising and is a circulatory stimulant.

Ginger	Eases tired muscles and is a warming oil. When it is hot outside you may not want to use this oil on your horse.
Grapefruit	This oil will help to disperse toxins, and lactic acid build up in the muscles.
Lavender	Good all-around muscle wash.
Marjoram	This oil is calming, good for stiffness, sprains, and joints.
Peppermint	This oil is good as a circulatory stimulant. It is a good all-around muscle wash. This works wells for easing painful muscles.
Roman Chamomile	Works with pains, sprains and helps as a sedative.
Sandalwood	Works wells for stiff joints and helps as a sedative.
Vetiver	Good for stiff joints and general pain. Also helps as a sedative.

Skinner's deep muscle massage

Roman Chamomile – 1 drop

Vetiver – 2 drops

Ylang-Ylang – 2 drops

Fractionated Coconut Oil – 10 drops

Printed in the United States
By Bookmasters